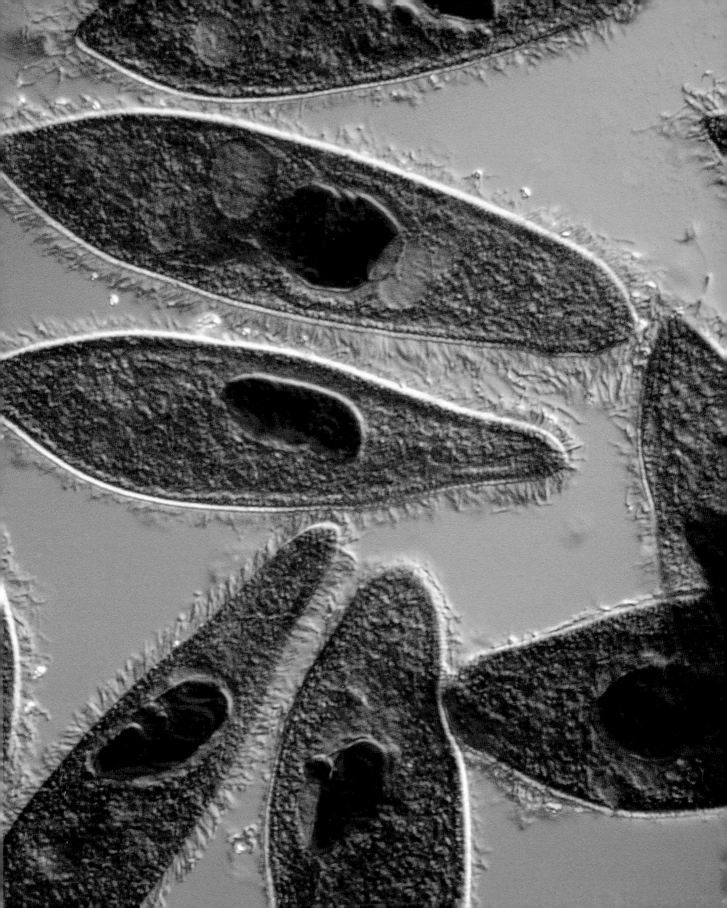

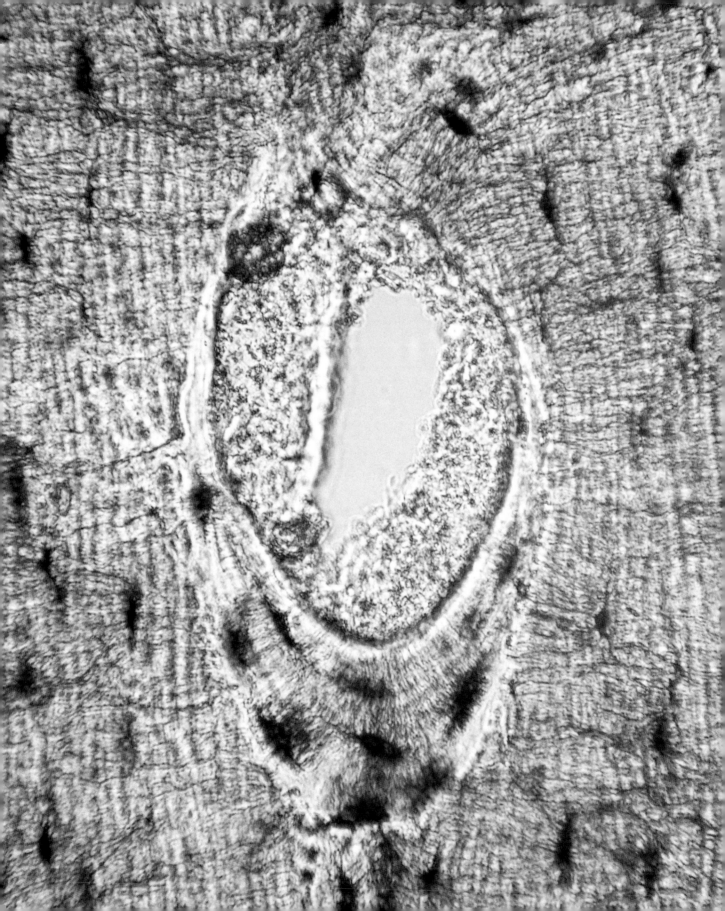

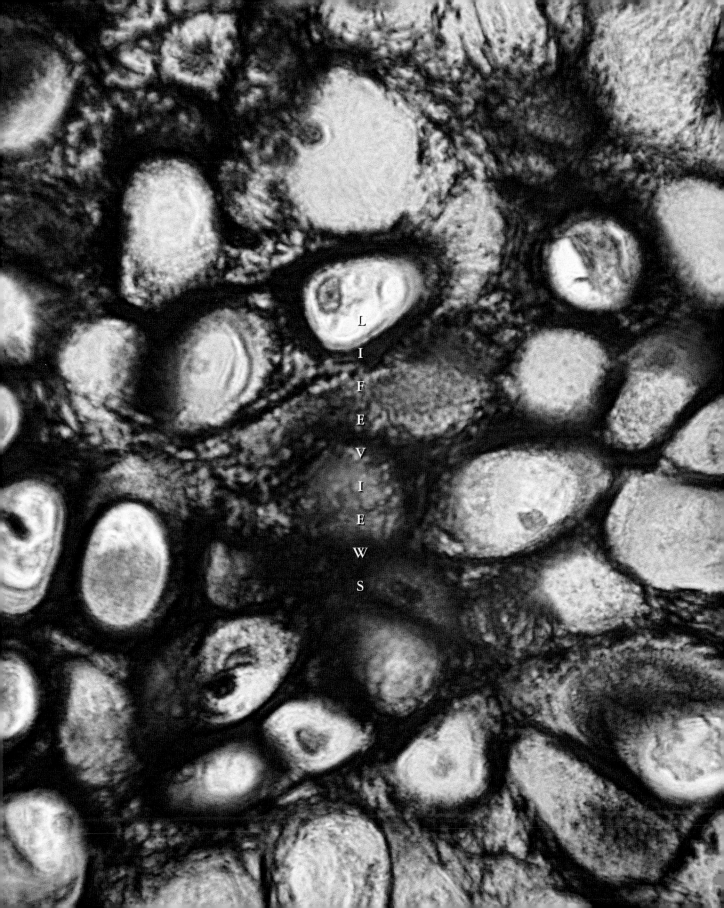

L I F E V I E W S

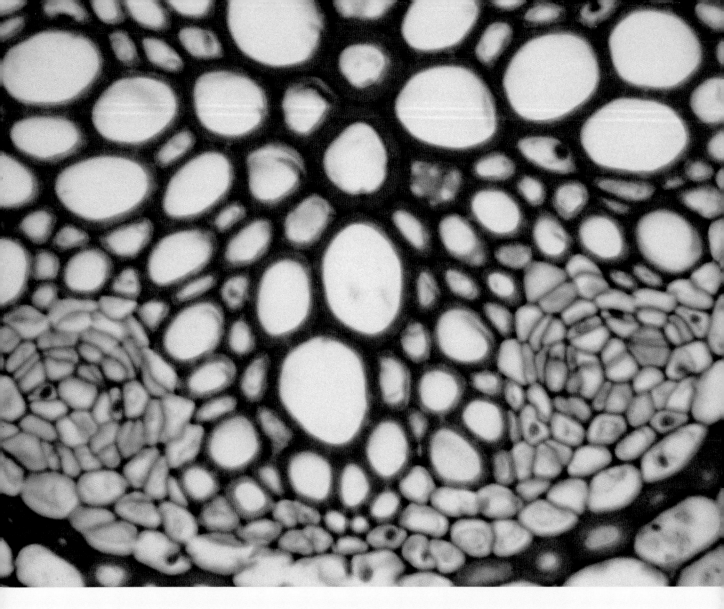

Published by Creative Education
123 South Broad Street, Mankato, Minnesota 56001
Creative Education is an imprint of The Creative Company

Art direction by Rita Marshall; Production design by The Design Lab

Photographs by JLM Visuals (David Balkwill, Richard P. Jacobs, David Wacker, Michael L. Womack), Tom Pantages (NASA), Photo Researchers (Michael Abbey/Science Source, Juergen Berger/Max-Planck Institute/Science Photo Library, Biophoto Associates/Science Source, Dr. Yorgo Nikas/Science Photo Library, Quest/Science Photo Library), Rainbow (Dan McCoy, Hank Morgan, James Sullivan), Tom Stack & Associates (E.J. Cable, Brian Parker, Tom Stack)

Library of Congress Cataloging-in-Publication Data

George, Michael.
Cells / by Michael George.
p. cm. — (LifeViews)
Summary: Discusses the formation, traits, and functions of various kinds of cells in living organisms.
ISBN 1-58341-245-X
1. Cells—Juvenile literature. [1. Cells.] I. Title. II. Series.
QH582.5 .G462   2002
571.6—dc21   2001047899

First Edition

2 4 6 8 9 7 5 3 1

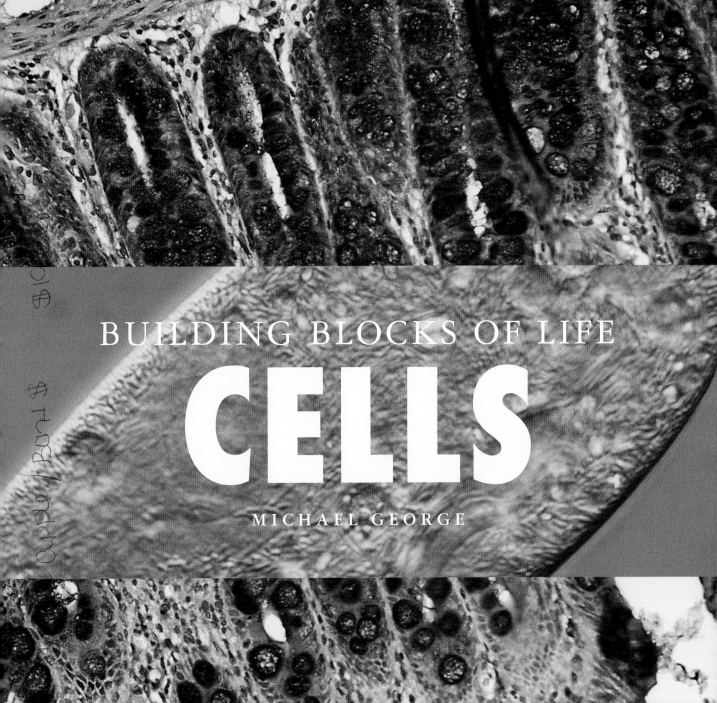

BUILDING BLOCKS OF LIFE

CELLS

MICHAEL GEORGE

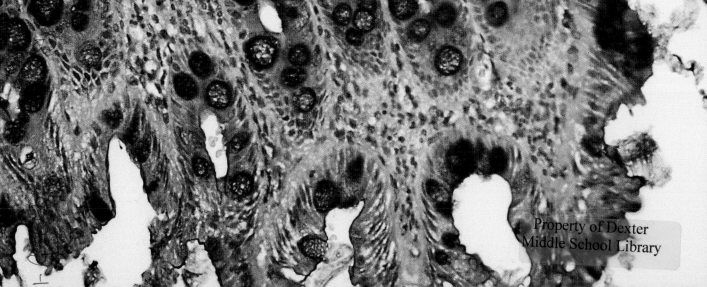

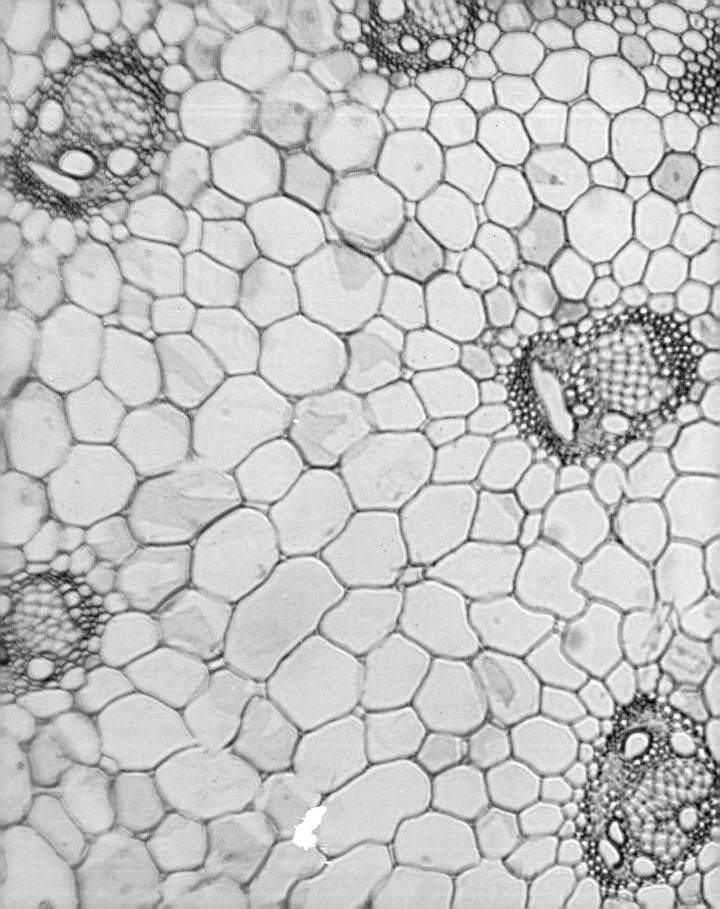

THE PLANET EARTH

is overflowing with life. Wherever we look, there are living **organisms**—trees, birds, fish, and even some creatures that are too small to be seen. All living things have a particular size, shape, and way of life. Yet despite the great variety of life on Earth, all organisms have many things in common. In particular, they are all made of the same basic building blocks, called **cells**.

Until about 300 years ago, no one realized that living organisms are made of cells. Most cells are simply too small to see with the naked eye. An average-sized cell is about one-thousandth of an inch wide. It would take about 32 of

Cells are the "bricks" with which all life is made.

these cells to fill the period at the end of this sentence.

In the late 1600s, Anton van Leeuwenhoek constructed the world's first high-powered **microscope**. It magnified the images of objects to nearly 300 times their normal size. Using his microscope, Leeuwenhoek peered into the world of little things. He made some startling discoveries. When he placed a drop of rainwater under the microscope, he saw tiny creatures swimming about. When he looked at a drop of blood, he saw countless saucer-shaped blobs. And when he examined a piece of skin, he saw something that resembled the bricks in a cobblestone road. Without knowing it, Leeuwenhoek was the first person to see cells.

Since the time of Leeuwenhoek, scientists have determined that all living things are made of cells. The simplest organisms consist of a single, solitary cell. These tiny creatures, called **microbes**, can be found in the air, in a drop of

Microscopes enable scientists to study the human body in minute detail, from red blood cells (top), which carry oxygen and carbon dioxide to and from tissues, to the waste-managing cells of the large intestine (bottom).

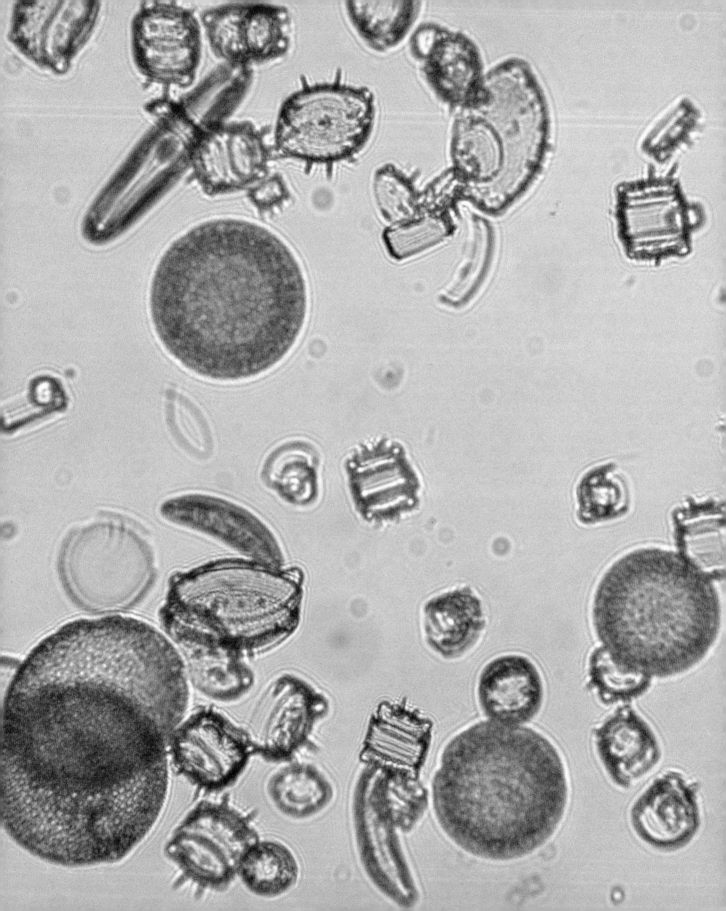

pond water, and at the bottom of the ocean. They live in frozen glaciers and in scorching deserts. Some one-celled organisms even live in our hair, on our skin, and inside different parts of our bodies.

Amazingly, a one-celled organism can do many of the things that a human body can do. It can make or catch food, eliminate wastes, grow, and react to changes in the environment. A one-celled organism can even reproduce. By dividing, the single cell becomes two.

One-celled organisms are responsible for many of the changes we see in the world. Microbes that live on the ground eat dead plants and animals, causing them to **decay** and turn into nutrient-rich soil. Microbes that live in the air settle on exposed food. They can make food change color and smell bad. Microbes that live on a person's body can cause cuts to turn red and become infected.

Paramecia belong to a large group of one-celled microorganisms called protozoans. Found in freshwater, paramecia move by means of tiny hairs called cilia, unlike one-celled algae (left), which cannot move on their own.

Unlike microbes, most of the organisms that we see every day contain many cells. Small plants and animals contain billions of cells. Our own bodies are made up of about 100 trillion cells. Larger organisms, such as elephants or sequoia trees, contain even more cells than this.

Plants and animals contain many different kinds of cells, each type performing a specific job. Some of the cells in many-celled organisms are designed for protection. One type of protective cell is **leaf epidermis,** found on the outside of leaves. Leaf epidermis cells fit together like the pieces of a jigsaw puzzle. They are covered with a waxy, waterproof coating that prevents leaves from drying out. Leaf epidermis cells also protect leaves from dangerous germs and injury.

People also have epidermis cells, better known as skin cells. Skin cells are thin and flat. They are stacked upon each other like pancakes. It takes billions of skin cells to cover a person's whole body. A person has more than 10 million skin cells on his or her hand alone. Like leaf epidermis cells, skin cells prevent our bodies from drying out and protect us from germs and injury.

Cells vary in shape depending upon their function. Leaf (left), onion (middle), and seaweed (right) epidermis cells form flat "walls" to protect plants from harm. Root cells (top), responsible for growth, are often round and clustered.

When we have a cut or a scratch, germs can get past our bodies' skin cells. If this happens, another type of cell comes to the rescue. These cells, called **leukocytes**, look like formless blobs of jelly. They can actually change shape, enabling them to surround and engulf dangerous germs. Leukocytes die after destroying many germs. They collect near infections and become visible as pus.

In order for plants and animals to grow to any stature, they need some method of support. All plant cells have a built-in method of support: they are surrounded by a rigid covering called a **cell wall**. The cell wall makes plant cells stiff and strong. Trees and other woody plants have special cells with extra-thick cell walls. These cells give trees additional support, enabling them to grow high above the ground.

Unlike plant cells, animal cells are not reinforced by cell walls. Most animal cells are soft and flexible. As a result, animals need special cells to support their bodies. The framework of your body, your skeleton, is made up of **bone** cells. Bone cells are surrounded by a hard material that makes bone stiff and strong.

Lacking rigid cell walls, most animal cells are quite pliable.

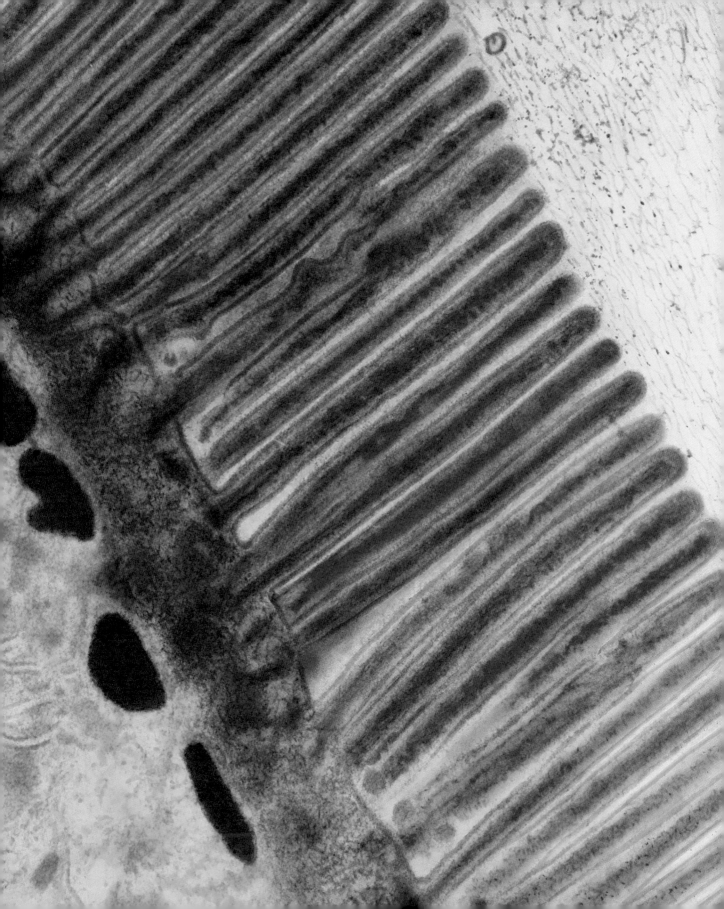

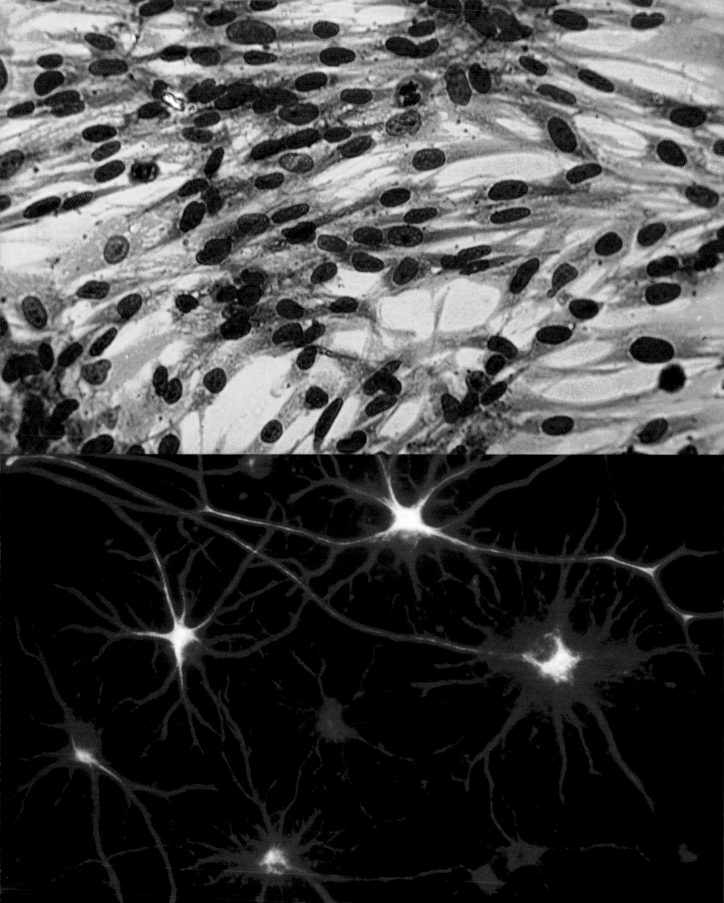

Cartilage cells, which form the gristle on the end of a chicken bone, also provide animals with support.

Animals also have cells designed for movement. Movement is accomplished by **muscle** cells, long, thin cells that can contract. When a group of muscle cells contracts, it pulls on your bones and causes your arm, leg, or fingers to move. Muscle cells enable you to run, throw a baseball, or write your name. There are also muscle cells that you cannot control. Among other things, these cells are responsible for the occasional rumbling of your stomach and the constant beating of your heart.

Nerve cells, or **neurons**, are another important type of animal cell. They transmit all sorts of messages through your body. Neurons in your hand tell you if something is hot or cold. Those in your eyes help you see the colors of a sunset. Neurons in your mouth and nose help you taste a hot-fudge sundae and smell the scent of a rose. Your body also contains neurons whose messages are not so obvious. These cells control your heartbeat, breathing, and many other processes that you are not always aware of.

Beneath the billions of skin cells (top) covering a human body lies a complex network of neurons (bottom). A neuron's small branches (dendrites) receive electrical signals, while its large branch (axon) conducts them to other nerve cells.

Like one-celled organisms, the cells in your body need food to survive. In many-celled organisms, individual cells cannot go out and find their own food. Instead, **nutrients** must be transported to each cell. In most animals, food is dissolved in the bloodstream and is transported to each and every cell. The cells absorb the food and use it to fuel their activities.

In order to function, animal cells also need a constant supply of oxygen. Oxygen is carried through your bloodstream by special cells called **red blood cells**. Red blood cells are shaped like smooth saucers, enabling them to flow through thin veins and arteries without getting stuck. Your body contains an enormous number of red blood cells—a single drop of blood contains more than five million.

As we have learned, Anton van Leeuwenhoek was the first person to see a cell. He used microscopes that magnified objects to about 300 times their normal size. With them, he could see microbes and skin cells, bone cells, and blood cells. However, the microscopes that Leeuwenhoek used were nothing like the ones that scientists use today. In modern laboratories, scientists

All cells need food to survive. The cells of a chicken embryo (top) absorb the nutrients they need for growth from the egg yolk. Human cells, such as gastrointestinal cells (bottom), feed on nutrients dissolved in the bloodstream.

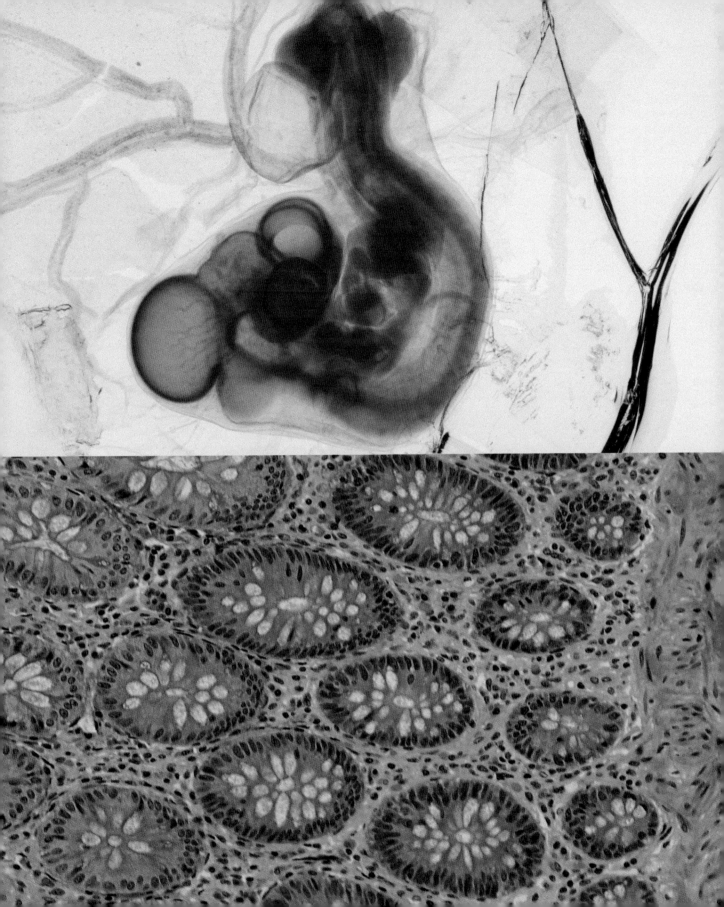

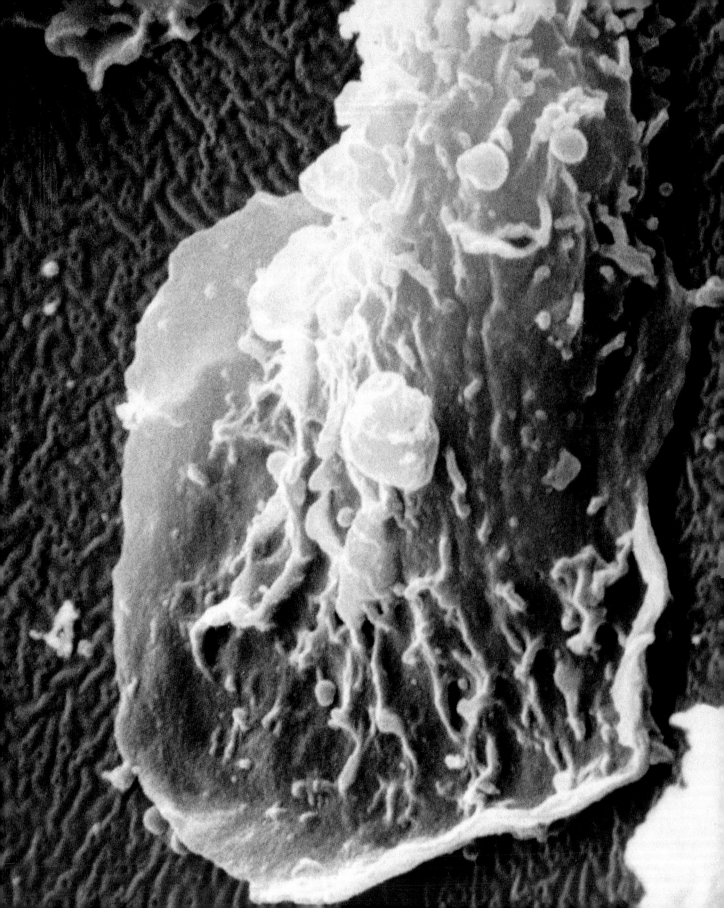

use microscopes that magnify objects to more than one million times their normal size. With today's microscopes, scientists can see *inside* cells.

Although cells differ in many ways, they also share many traits. Whether it is a one-celled organism or a cell in your own body, every cell is separated from the rest of the world by an extremely thin covering called the **cell membrane**. Like the skin that covers your body, the cell membrane separates the cell from the outside environment. This membrane, however, is more like a gate than a solid barrier. Equipped with tiny pores, the cell membrane regulates everything that enters and leaves the cell. It allows certain nutrients, gases, and liquids to pass into the cell, and keeps dangerous materials out.

Inside the cell membrane is a grayish, jelly-like substance called **cytoplasm**. The cytoplasm in most cells consists largely of water, but also contains small amounts of salt, vitamins, and minerals. Also floating throughout the cytoplasm of many cells are tiny structures called **organelles**, meaning "little organs." Like the organs of the human body, each

White blood cells, or leukocytes, have one function: to fight infection. Once alerted to invading pathogens, such as disease-causing bacteria, the leukocytes attack, absorbing them through their cell membranes and destroying them.

organelle performs a specific activity. One type of organelle digests food. Another packages and transports nutrients. There are also organelles that supply energy for the cell's activities and ones that destroy dangerous germs.

The biggest, most obvious structure in most cells is called the **nucleus**. The nucleus is the cell's control center. It contains all the information about what the cell is and what it will be. The nucleus controls the various organelles and issues instructions for most of the cell's activities.

Within each cell, the most basic processes of life take place. Cells digest food, eliminate wastes, produce energy, and respond to their surroundings. They also **reproduce**. A one-celled organism periodically divides, so that there are two cells where once there was only one. But where do the trillions of cells that form a tree, a fish, a bird, or a person come from?

Amazingly, all many-celled organisms begin life as a single cell. The cell from which you originated contained all the instructions on how you were to be made. It contained the

Despite their varied shapes and sizes, all plant and animal cells are tiny bits of life, capable of functioning as independent units. The scientific study of cell structure, growth, behavior, and reproduction is called cytology.

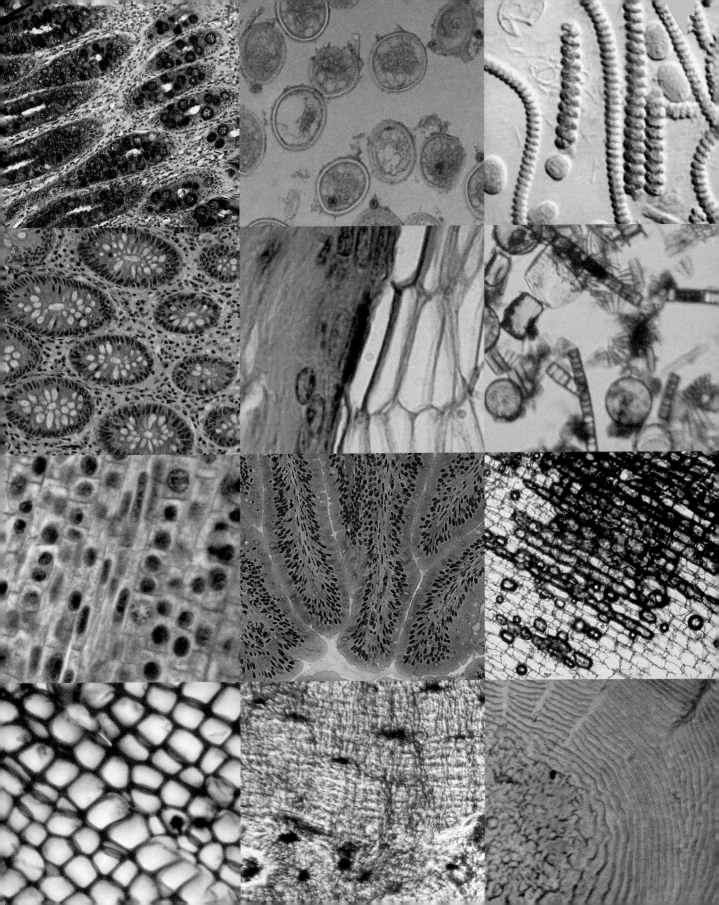

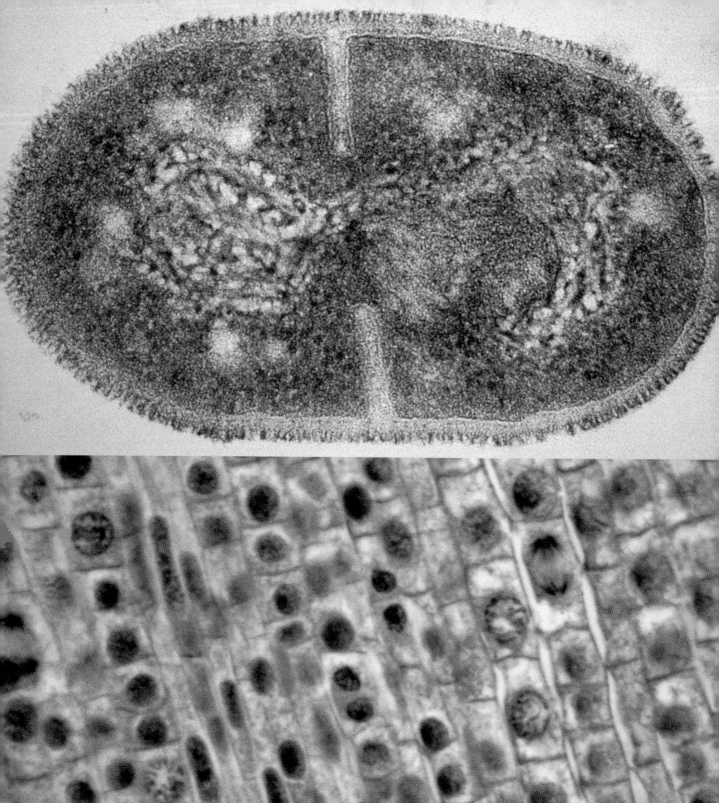

information for how many fingers you should have, where your legs should be, the shape of your head, and everything else that makes you a human being.

Following these instructions, the cell from which you originated divided, similar to the way a one-celled organism reproduces. Rather than separating, however, the resulting two cells remained attached to each other. After a short time, the two cells divided again, forming four cells. Time after time, the increasing number of cells contin-ued to divide.

At some point in your development, your cells began to **differentiate**. Some became skin cells, some muscle cells, some nerve cells, and so on. Eventually, the different types of cells grouped together. Skin cells combined into skin, muscle cells into muscles, and nerve cells into nerves. Together, all the differ-ent cells formed you.

Throughout your entire life, cells in your body continue

A one-celled microorganism, such as a bacterium (top), reproduces by splitting into two independent cells. This process is called fission. Plant cells (bottom) also divide but remain attached to one another.

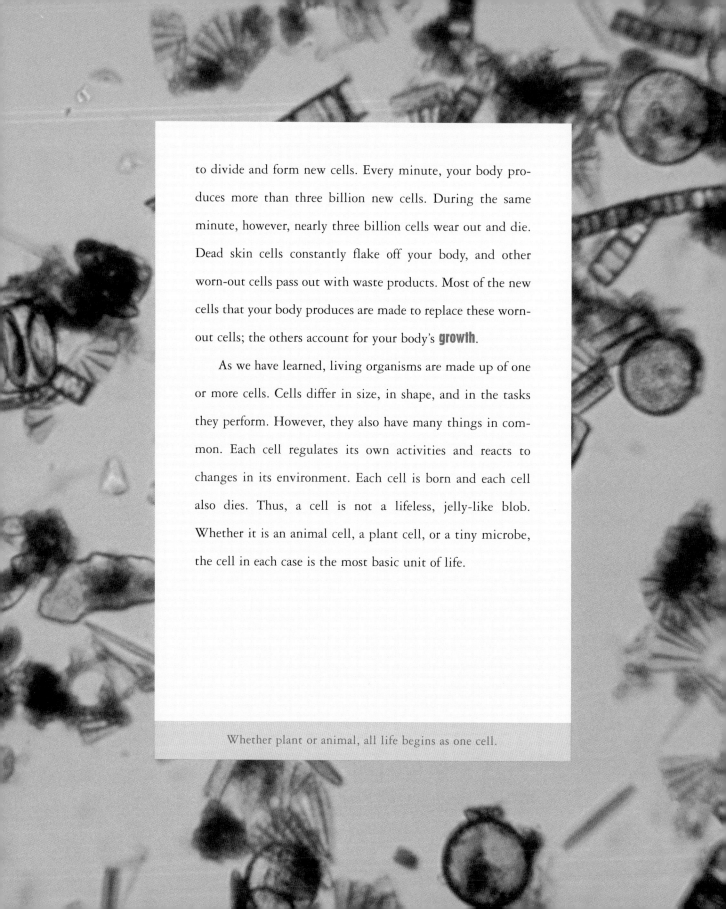

to divide and form new cells. Every minute, your body produces more than three billion new cells. During the same minute, however, nearly three billion cells wear out and die. Dead skin cells constantly flake off your body, and other worn-out cells pass out with waste products. Most of the new cells that your body produces are made to replace these worn-out cells; the others account for your body's **growth**.

As we have learned, living organisms are made up of one or more cells. Cells differ in size, in shape, and in the tasks they perform. However, they also have many things in common. Each cell regulates its own activities and reacts to changes in its environment. Each cell is born and each cell also dies. Thus, a cell is not a lifeless, jelly-like blob. Whether it is an animal cell, a plant cell, or a tiny microbe, the cell in each case is the most basic unit of life.

Whether plant or animal, all life begins as one cell.

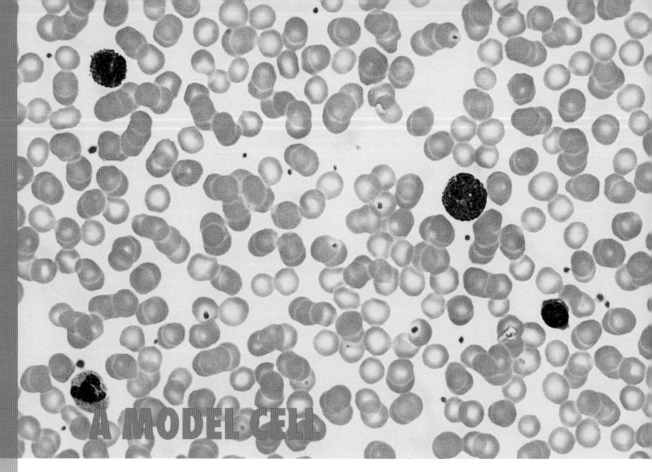

A MODEL CELL

Because the average-sized cell is about one-thousandth of an inch wide, cells are best viewed with a microscope. This activity, however, will show you how to make a cell model as large as your hand so you can easily view all of its parts.

You Will Need

- One package of sparkling white grape gelatin mix
- A measuring cup
- A sealable (zipping) plastic sandwich bag
- A handful of plain M&M's* in a variety of colors
- A spoon
- A mixing bowl
- Club soda
- A refrigerator
- A large grape

Making the Model

1. Mix the gelatin according to the directions on the package, but do not put it in the refrigerator to chill.
2. Let the gelatin cool to room temperature, then have a friend help you pour it into the sandwich bag. Do not fill the bag to the top. Leave about an inch (2.5 cm) of empty space below the sealing strips.

* M&M's is a registered trademark of Mars, Incorporated.

3. Seal the bag tightly and put it in the refrigerator. Chill until firm (about three hours).

4. Now open the bag and push the grape into the center of the gelatin. Push the M&M's in at varying distances from the center.

5. Seal the bag tightly and place it on a table or countertop.

Observation

You now have a model of the type of cell found in eukaryotic organisms, or higher plants and animals. The plastic sandwich bag represents the cell's membrane. Unlike the plastic bag, a true cell membrane allows gases and liquids to pass through it. Some cell membranes are so thin that they are barely visible, even under a microscope.

The gelatin represents the cell's cytoplasm, the jelly-like substance that surrounds and cushions the nucleus (the grape). The M&M's are the cell's organelles, the membrane-enclosed structures that act like the organs in your body. Some organelles (the green M&M's, for example) may process food like a stomach. Others (the brown M&M's, for example) may fight infection.

If you gently squeeze your cell model, you'll notice that it moves and changes shape. Most of the cells in your body respond this same way. Bone cells are an exception. They are surrounded by a hard material that makes bones stiff and strong.

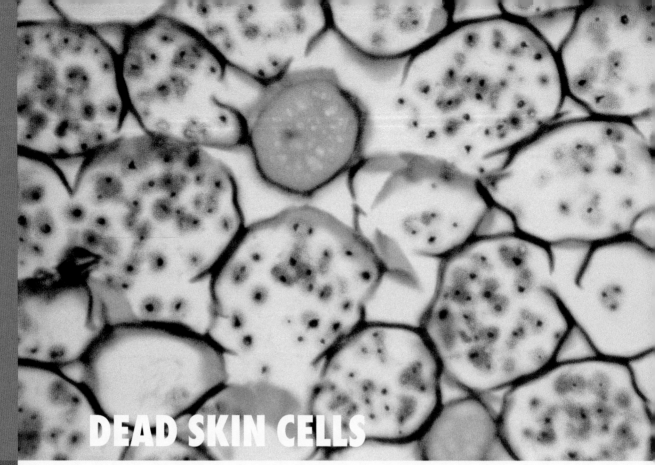

DEAD SKIN CELLS

Your skin's outer layer of cells is called the epidermis. These cells protect your body against germs and injury, and help keep it from drying out. If you've ever gotten a sunburn, you've seen your epidermal cells in action. When your skin started to peel, your body was shedding thin layers of dead skin cells to make way for the new cells that had already formed underneath.

Epidermal cells are constantly being replaced as old cells die and flake off. In fact, nearly 95 percent of the skin you can see is made up of dead skin cells. To watch some of these cells being shed, first find a room with a curtained window through which the sun is shining brightly. Close the curtains until just a narrow beam of light shines into the room. Can you see the dust particles floating in the air?

Now hold your arm in the light and scratch the top of it. You should see quite a few more particles rise into the air. These particles are dead skin cells. Every time you move, you lose more of them. It may not be a pleasant thought, but dead skin cells make up about 80 percent of the dust in your home!

LEARN MORE ABOUT CELLS

The American Society for Cell Biology
8120 Woodmont Avenue, Suite 750
Bethesda, MD 20814
http://www.ascb.org

The Biology Project: Cell Biology
(Internet site created by the
  University of Arizona)
http://www.biology.arizona.edu/cell_bio/
  cell_bio.html

The British Society for Cell Biology
Department of Zoology
Downing Street
Cambridge CB2 3EJ, United Kingdom
http://www.bscb.org

Cells Alive!
(a visual online tour of cells)
http://www.cellsalive.com

Eureka! Science Corporation
P.O. Box 42615
Indianapolis, IN 46242
http://www.eurekascience.com/ICanDoThat/
  index.htm

Kapili.com: Cells
(online resource for cell information)
http://www.kapili.com/c/cell.html

Microbe
(microbe news site supported by the
  American Society for Microbiology)
http://www.microbe.org

INDEX

Microbes were the first forms of life on Earth.